T0113312

Walking
With the
King

*Through the Reality
of God's Love*

ELEANOR STOCKERT

WESTBOW
PRESS®
A DIVISION OF THOMAS NELSON
& ZONDERVAN

All scriptures are taken from the New King James Version
of the Bible, unless otherwise indicated.

Scripture taken from THE AMPLIFIED BIBLE, Old Testament copyright
1965, 1987 by the Zondervan Corporation. The Amplified New Testament
copyright 1958, 1987 by The Lockman Foundation. Used by permission.

Scripture quotations marked NLT are taken from the *Holy Bible,* New Living Translation,
copyright 1996, 2004, 2007 by Tyndale House Foundation. Used by permission of
Tyndale House Publishers, Inc., Carol Stream, Illinois 60188. All rights reserved.

WestBow Press books may be ordered through booksellers or by contacting:

WestBow Press
A Division of Thomas Nelson & Zondervan
1663 Liberty Drive
Bloomington, IN 47403
www.westbowpress.com
1 (866) 928-1240

ISBN: 978-1-5127-3829-2 (sc)
ISBN: 978-1-5127-3830-8 (e)

Library of Congress Control Number: 2016905830

Print information available on the last page.

WestBow Press rev. date: 4/15/2016

Contents

Dedication

To my wonderful great-grandchildren:
Mackenzie, Sage, Peighton, Westin and Rocky.
I love you all!

In Appreciation

To Marty Blair, my very special friend and prayer partner
for so many years. You are truly a
blessing from God and I could
have never written these books without you. May the
Lord richly bless you and your wonderful family.

Introduction

I've been a Christian since 1975 and for much of that time I walked far below my privileges in Christ. The reason I am writing this book is to share the principles that Holy Spirit has taught me that have opened the door to experiencing the abundant life Jesus promised us (John 10:10).

God's grace and love are so amazing that even after the fall of mankind in the Garden of Eden He immediately put a plan into motion to restore His earth and His family to the way He originally created them. The magnitude of His Love for us can be seen by what He gave up to get us restored. God gave His only Son to die in our place for our sins (John 3:16).

Father God's greatest desire is that we would be conformed to the image of His Son Jesus (Romans 8:29). That can only be achieved when we receive His love. I John 4:16 says it is one thing to know about God's love but another to actually believe in it. It is only in knowing *and* believing in His love that positions us to be transformed into the image of Jesus. It is then that our lives are a demonstration of His love in all we say and do.

How do we get to that point in our lives of being a demonstration of His love? One of the greatest revelations I have received concerns the connection between receiving (knowing and believing) God's love for me and the releasing of His power in my life. Ephesians 3:14-21 shows us how the connection works; ... that Christ would dwell in our hearts through faith and that we would be rooted and grounded in God's love to such a degree that we would experience the Love of Christ. Through experiencing the Love of Christ we would be made complete with all the fullness of life and power that comes from God. This passage continues by saying that once we get a revelation of God's love, then we are in a position for God to do great and miraculous things in us and through us for His glory. I John 4:18 says that "perfected love casts out fear." In His love we become mature believers who are so secure in God's love that we do not respond to fear; and without fear the enemy cannot work in our lives.

Walking with the King – living conformed to the image of Jesus – is God's perfect will for all of His children. Many believers never reach that place in their journey of spiritual development. Many accept Jesus as Savior but never make Him Lord of their lives. Others make Him Lord but never develop their faith to the point they believe scriptures like John 17:23 which tells us that God the Father loves us just as much as He loves Jesus. Spiritual maturity comes when we make a quality decision to believe what God's Word says regardless of what other people say or what our own feelings tell us. It requires an act of our will to believe what He says about us, to do the things He says we can do and to receive everything He has given to us according to His Word. It takes a quality decision on our part to lay down the low life (our worldly ways) and receive the high life (God's ways) (Matthew 10:39). The Bible says that the Kingdom of God is within us (Luke 17:21). His Kingdom is ruled by Love because Jesus is on the throne of our hearts operating through our lives. As we receive God's love for us and allow that love to flow outward into the lives of others, our walk with the King grows stronger and stronger and we are changed from glory to glory (II Corinthians 3:18).

We must also be aware that this life Jesus died to give us does not come without opposition or a fight. It involves having unshakeable faith in the goodness of God so that we can stay strong when it looks like what we are believing for is not coming to pass. We need to remind ourselves that while there is a fight involved, it is a "good fight" because Jesus has already defeated the devil (Colossians 2:15). Our fight is only to enforce the defeat of the enemy and it comes by simply believing that Jesus will do what He said He would do in His Word (John 6:28).

To many believers walking with the King seems like a distant dream. While it may seem like a dream, it is a promise placed in the heart of every believer by the King Himself. Our part is to take ownership of that dream by faith and allow the Holy Spirit freedom to bring about the necessary changes in our lives that will cause us to be more Christ-like. As that happens we will bring great honor to God and He in turn will honor and bestow His favor on us (Jeremiah 33:9 NLT). Then the world will be able to see that we are truly **"walking with the King"**!

God's Amazing Plan

"Give thanks to the Lord for He is good! His faithful love endures forever." (Psalm 118:1 NLT)

I believe the major key to unlocking our understanding of God and His Word is found in our ability to know and receive His love. If we could only see ourselves the way the Lord sees us. I'll never forget the day I found the scripture that says that God the Father loves me just as much as He loves Jesus (John 17:23 NLT).

When we come to realize the love God has for us all fear will be gone! In Ephesians 3:16–19 (NLT) Paul is praying for the Church:

> ¹⁶ I pray that from his glorious, unlimited resources he will empower you with inner strength through his Spirit. ¹⁷ Then Christ will make his home in your hearts as you trust in him. Your roots will grow down into God's love and keep you strong. ¹⁸ And may you have the power to understand, as all God's people should, how wide, how long, how high, and how deep his love is. ¹⁹ May you experience the love of Christ, though it is too

great to understand fully. Then you will be made complete with all the fullness of life and power that comes from God.

Ephesians 3:20 explains the fruit of receiving God's love:

> [20] Now to Him who is able to do exceedingly abundantly above all that we ask or think, according to the power that works in us,

God's power is able to work in us because our love is perfected in Him (I John 4:18) and without fear we can confidently trust in Him to work all things for our good in our lives (Romans 8:28). Knowing and believing that God is love allows us to be able to see the amazing future He has planned for us.

Knowing and believing that God is love also allows us to see His great love in His Word from Genesis to Revelation. Long before the earth was created, our Heavenly Father had an overwhelming desire to have a family. True love can never be satisfied unless it is constantly giving. At this time God's love was showered on His Only Son, Jesus Christ. The Holy Spirit was present as well as all the angels. The angels, however, were merely servants and they were "programmed" to carry out what they were told to do. Father God wanted someone like Himself whom He could love and who would choose to freely love Him in return.

I believe that because Jesus loved His Father so much and because He understood the desire of His Father's heart to have a family to love, He called a meeting with the Father and the Holy Spirit. I believe they devised a plan to fulfill that dream. That dream would be manifested in the creation of Man – a being with a free will who would of his own choosing be a recipient of God's never-ending love. Genesis 1:26 says, "Let us make man in our image." I'm sure the risk of such a plan was discussed. If Man rejected God he would leave himself open to the influence of Satan, God's enemy since having been kicked out of heaven (Ezekiel 28). That wrong choice would be devastating not only to Man but also to God. At that point I believe Jesus' love for His Father was shown. I believe that Jesus agreed that if Man ever made that wrong choice, He Himself would come to earth as a man to give mankind one more opportunity to receive God's love. This great plan of salvation would bring mankind back to God forever. This was the plan devised "before the foundations of the world ..." (Ephesians 1:4, I Peter 1:20).

When Father God created Adam and Eve., He prepared everything that they would ever need or desire, and He was very happy and satisfied that all that He had made was very good (Genesis 1:31). God and His creation fellowshipped in perfect love as they walked and talked together. His relationship with man was blessed until Satan entered the Garden of Eden in the form of a serpent and tempted man and undermined all that God had intended for man to do.

Man, who had been made in God's image and had been given authority over all things, lost everything to an evil power that would enslave him and all of humanity until Jesus Christ, God's Son, came to earth. This "second Adam" came and redeemed Man back to the Father by giving Himself as a sacrifice (I Corinthians 15:45-50). John 3:16 states, "For God so loved the world that He gave His only begotten Son, that whoever believes in Him should not perish but have everlasting life."

Father God has always wanted a people whom He could love and bless and one who would love and obey Him. The reason He has wanted Man to obey Him is not to rule over or enslave him. He has required man to obey Him because obedience brings the blessings of God; one of those being the protection of God. Man needs the protection of God for two reasons: one, to be kept safe from the devil, and two, to be kept safe when God deals with and destroys sin. God knows that the devil desires to destroy man by tempting him to disobey God. Satan is continually trying to keep man in disobedience to what God says so that he can steal, kill and destroy according to John 10:10. Sin tainted the Garden of Eden because of Adam and Eve's disobedience (Genesis 2:17). Throughout the Old Testament God continually reached out to man warning him to turn away from sin and promising to protect him when His wrath was poured out on the wickedness in the earth. For example, the Lord warned and warned the people through Noah, but they would not listen to him (II Peter 2:5). God had to keep His Word so He saved Noah and his family and everyone else died in the flood (Genesis 7:1). God was not pouring out His wrath on people; He was pouring out His wrath on the sin which the people refused to rid themselves of. People look at these incidents in the Bible and mistakenly see a God who is cruel. But that is just not so! The Lord does not want any to perish (II Peter 3:9). There is always a reason behind all that the Lord does, and the motivation behind the reason is always LOVE. Concerning Noah, God flooded the earth to keep the blood line clean from which Jesus descended. A perfect sacrifice was needed to redeem mankind, so for Jesus to be the Savior of the world the sin that had penetrated the lineage had to be destroyed.

When Jesus died and was resurrected sin was forever defeated. Mankind entered into a dispensation of Grace, meaning that anyone who acknowledges Jesus Christ as Lord and Savior had his sins forgiven. Unlike in the Old Testament where sins were atoned for by the sacrificing of animals, in this dispensation of Grace, sins are remitted – completely wiped away by the blood sacrifice of God's only Son (Romans 3:22-25).

The need for obedience to God's Word will be just as important in the end times as it was in the Old Testament. Jesus said in John 14:15, "If you love me, keep my commandments." Once again, God's purpose for obedience is to open the door to His protection in an increasingly dangerous world. The days in which we are living are filled with corruption, immorality, and, perhaps most importantly, an increasing apathy toward all the evil that surrounds us. While God has been waiting patiently giving

Man every opportunity to receive Jesus, there is coming a point in time when the opportunity to be a part of the overcoming Church, a church without spot or wrinkle (Ephesians 5:27), will be gone. And, according to the Bible, that time is coming very soon. Jesus said that no man would know the day or the hour – only God the Father knows – but we would know the season. All prophecy in the Bible points to the time in which we are living as the time when Jesus will come back to take His people home to be with Him forever. This time is referred to as the "rapture" or the catching away of the Church. The only people who will be going in it will be people who are walking very closely to the Lord and totally prepared for His return.

After the rapture takes place, Satan will go on a rampage as never before. With the Church gone, there will be no one to check his power. II Thessalonians 2:1-10 (excluding vs. 2,5,8) says,

> [1] Now, brethren, concerning the coming of our Lord Jesus Christ and our gathering together to Him (rapture) [3] Let no one deceive you by any means; for *that Day will not come* unless the falling away comes first, and the man of sin is revealed, the son of perdition, [4] who opposes and exalts himself above all that is called God or that is worshiped, so that he sits as God in the temple of God, showing himself that he is God. [6] And now you know what is restraining, that he may be revealed in his own time. [7] For the mystery of lawlessness is already at work; only He who now restrains *will do so* until He is taken out of the way. [9] The coming of the *lawless one* is according to the working of Satan, with all power, signs, and lying wonders, [10] and with all unrighteous deception among those who perish, because they did not receive the love of the truth, that they might be saved.

Satan will try to do what he's always wanted to do – be God. That's why he and a third of the angels who rebelled along with him were cast out of heaven (Ezekiel 28). He will create a "trinity" – a counterfeit of the "The Holy Trinity – the Father, the Son and the Holy Spirit." The evil trinity will consist of Satan, the Antichrist and the False Prophet. The False Prophet will always direct attention to the Antichrist in the same way Holy Spirit directs believers to our Lord Jesus.

While Satan will be operating unchecked during the first three and one-half years of the tribulation, God, through His Love and Mercy, will still be reaching out to all mankind. His mercy will be poured out on those lukewarm believers who did not make the first rapture and on the many that will be saved during the tribulation. The Antichrist will constantly be after these believers seeking to destroy them, and he will be successful in killing many of them. After a three-and-half-year period, those remaining alive will be taken out in a mid-tribulation rapture, before Almighty God's wrath is poured out on the earth. If we fail to heed his admonition, we will have to suffer the consequences of being disobedient. Revelation 3:15-16,19 warns,

> [15] "I know your works, that you are neither cold nor hot. could wish you were cold or hot. [16] So then, because you are lukewarm, and neither cold nor hot, I will vomit you out of My mouth. [19] As many as I love, I rebuke and chasten. Therefore be zealous and repent

After the seven years of tribulation, believers will return with Jesus to be with Him at the battle of Armageddon where Jesus will conquer all the armies of the Antichrist. He will then set up His earthly kingdom with His people (us!!), ruling and reigning with Him for a thousand years.

Throughout the entire book of Revelation, God is calling

people to repent and accept Jesus as Lord and Savior. His long suffering is so great that even at the end of the millennium – that one thousand-year period when Satan is bound and Jesus will rule – Satan will be released to give people one last chance to choose to follow Jesus or Satan (Revelation 20:7-8). While it is hard to believe that there could be anyone who would choose to follow Satan after living during the millennium with Christ there will be those who do just that. At that time Satan and all those who have followed him down through the ages will be cast into the lake of fire, where they, along with the Antichrist and the False Prophet, will be tormented forever.

For those who received Jesus the celebrating will have just begun. We will praise our wonderful Heavenly Father as He arrives in that Holy City, New Jerusalem. There we will spend eternity with Jesus and His dearly beloved family. That is what Father God's magnificent plan was from the beginning. He always wanted a family that He could love and bless and one that would love and bless Him. From the start, the blessings of God came through obedience, and in the end times, it is obedience that will bring about the final blessing – being caught away with our Savior when He returns for His Bride, the Church. Determine to be obedient to the admonition Jesus gave in Revelation 22:16 & 20:

> [16] "I, Jesus, have sent My angel to testify to you these things in the churches. I am the Root and the Offspring of David, the Bright and Morning Star … [20] He who testifies to these things says, 'Surely I am coming quickly.'" Amen.

Jesus is the King of Kings and Lord of Lords! As we are obedient to prepare for His coming, our reply to the Lord's last words will echo those of the apostle John:

Even so, come, Lord Jesus!

Our Father

Our Heavenly Father is a good God! To know Him is to love Him! Psalm 145:8–17 (NLT) tells us just how wonderful He is:

⁸ The LORD is merciful and compassionate,
slow to get angry and filled with unfailing love.
⁹ The LORD is good to everyone.
He showers compassion on all his creation.
¹⁰ All of your works will thank you, LORD,
and your faithful followers will praise you.
¹¹ They will speak of the glory of your kingdom;
they will give examples of your power.
¹² They will tell about your mighty deeds
and about the majesty and glory of your reign.
¹³ For your kingdom is an everlasting kingdom.
You rule throughout all generations.
The LORD always keeps his promises;
he is gracious in all he does.
¹⁴ The LORD helps the fallen
and lifts those bent beneath their loads.

¹⁵ The eyes of all look to you in hope;
you give them their food as they need it.
¹⁶ When you open your hand,
you satisfy the hunger and thirst of every living thing.
¹⁷ The LORD is righteous in everything he does;
he is filled with kindness.

God loves us so much and longs for us to have an abundant life, full of His joy and blessings. But He really cannot accomplish much in our lives until we know His true nature. He wants us to realize that He is love; when the revelation of that takes hold in our hearts, when we not only know but believe in His love, then He is able to prosper us in every area of our lives. God's Word confirms this in Ephesians 3:19-20 (NLT):

> ¹⁹ May you experience the love of Christ, though it is too great to understand fully. Then you will be made complete with all the fullness of life and power that comes from God. ²⁰ Now all glory to God, who is able, through his mighty power at work within us, to accomplish infinitely more than we might ask or think.

When I believed and received Jesus Christ as my Savior and Lord in 1975, He saved me out of a life full of fear, grief, and depression. I felt so free and had such a hunger to know Him that I would read the Bible day and night. I would get so excited over the goodness of God and the promises I found in His Word for my life. My life changed so dramatically that in a matter of four months my husband and three daughters gave their lives to the Lord also!

As exciting as the beginning of my walk was with the Lord, I was confused by what I saw and heard in the pulpit. The church that we started attending was very troubling to me. The pastor was very kind and loving to me and my family but when he preached he seemed so different. He would look angry and pound the pulpit. As he did this I would look at the people in the congregation and they all seemed fearful. I would think to myself, something is very wrong here.

One Sunday morning an evangelist and his family came to preach. Just before he started his message he carried his four-year-old daughter in and laid her on the pew in front of him. She had major health problems and would whimper in pain occasionally. At one point in his message he turned and pointed to her and said, "God did this to teach me a lesson!" I thought to myself, what makes him so special that God would sacrifice the well-being of his daughter for him so he could learn something? Immediately from within I heard the words, "No, this is wrong!" But when I went home I began reasoning, thinking something must be wrong with me. I thought to myself that here is a pastor and evangelist, leaders in the church, and I'm just a new convert. Soon after this experience I believed God to baptize me in the Holy Spirit. The Word became so real to me and I knew I was right and the evangelist was wrong. I continued to search the scriptures looking for God's goodness. I found Romans 2:4 which states that it is the goodness of God that leads people to repentance (and brings changes into their lives).

I thank God that by His grace and the working of His mighty power through the Holy Spirit (My Helper) I learned that religious tradition was trying to rob me of my closeness to God. Jesus warns of this deception of the devil in Mark 7:13.

What was being taught in this church (and is still being taught today in many churches) is Old Testament Law and the religious traditions of men rather than the knowledge of God's Word. This kind of teaching annuls the grace and freedom we have in Christ. In Hosea 4:6a God says, "My people are destroyed for a lack of knowledge". The people in many churches today seem to know very little about what God says in His Word. They say that miracles have passed away and that God no longer heals today; only Jesus healed when he walked the earth. It is very sad because those whose belief system is based on the Law and tradition (who have rejected knowledge as Hosea 4:6b warns) are living far below the abundant life that Jesus promised for every area of their lives. Not only does this wrong-teaching affect those who believe it, but it also affects the unbelievers around them who have no desire to come to the Lord because of the powerless life they see believers living. They think that God is a harsh God, One Who has no power or compassion!

In order to really know our Heavenly Father we must diligently seek a revelation of Him through the leading of the Holy Spirit. In my early years as a Christian, I felt that I didn't really have the same closeness to Father God that I did to Jesus and Holy Spirit. We were taught about Jesus and Holy Spirit, but we were not taught that much about God, our "Father". We knew Him as Most High God. We knew to direct our prayers to Him in Jesus' Name. We knew to give God all the glory, honor and praise. But I wanted to know Him as my "Abba". Abba means "daddy" and denotes a relationship between a father and a child which stems from the father's love drawing him close. Romans 8:14–16 (NLT) states,

> [14] For all who are led by the Spirit of God are children of God. [15] So you have not received a spirit that makes you fearful slaves. Instead, you received God's Spirit when he adopted you as his own children. Now we call him, "Abba, Father."

> [16] For his Spirit joins with our spirit to affirm that we are God's children.

Ephesians 1:4–5 (NLT) reveals more about our Father's heart.

⁴ Even before he made the world, God loved us and chose us in Christ to be holy and without fault in his eyes. ⁵ God decided in advance to adopt us into his own family by bringing us to himself through Jesus Christ. This is what he wanted to do, and it gave him great pleasure.

After searching the scriptures, praying and meditating on the Word, I believe Holy Spirit has fulfilled my desire to know my Heavenly Father as "daddy" God. And the difference it has made in my relationship with Him has been life-changing.

For so long the world and much of the church has viewed God as a very old man seated on a throne with a very stern face, ready and eager to jump on people's mistakes and teach them lessons through tests and trials. People do believe in the love of God in that once a person has suffered enough, God delivers them. But it is a shaky love at best. For in the background there is always a question of what bad has to happen before the love of God is experienced. Satan knows that if he can frame the Love of God with fear, that he can keep the world from wanting anything to do with God and the Church from experiencing the loving nature of God.

In the world Satan has managed to get some of the most powerful businesses in the world – insurance companies – to legally declare disasters such as tornadoes, earthquakes and hurricanes as acts of God. They are not acts of God, but acts of Satan. In John 10:10 (AMP) Jesus says, "The thief comes only in order to steal and kill and destroy. I came that they may have *and* enjoy life, and have it in abundance (to the full, till it overflows)."

People in the world and some in the church have accused God our Father of terrible things. Pastors at gravesides of children have said things like, "God took this child because he needed another flower in His garden." Statements like this have turned many away from God. Whether they realize it or not, people who say such things are accusing God of working together with Satan in testing people. Satan is God's enemy! God is never tempted with evil nor does He tempt anyone with evil. The Bible is very clear about this and even warns us never to say it! James 1:13–17 (NLT) states,

> [13] And remember, when you are being tempted, do not say, "God is tempting me." God is never tempted to do wrong, and he never tempts anyone else. [14] Temptation comes from our own desires, which entice us and drag us away. [15] These desires give birth to sinful actions. And when sin is allowed to grow, it gives birth to death. [16] So don't be misled, my dear brothers and sisters. [17] Whatever is good and perfect is a gift coming down to us from God our Father, who created all the lights in the heavens. He never changes or casts a shifting shadow.

It is only in understanding and receiving God's love, and knowing and believing that His desire for our lives is all good that we can have full confidence in Him. When that happens He is able to make us like Jesus so we can take His love to a lost and dying world. God's message to a lost world has always been the same and can be found in Jeremiah 29:11 (NLT): [11] For I know the plans I have for you," says the LORD. "They are plans for good and not for disaster, to give you a future and a hope. When God created Man He said, "Let us make man in our image according to our likeness" (Gen. 1:26). According to this scripture we are to look like Him and act and be like Him. God is a speaking Spirit. He creates with His words. We likewise are speaking spirits and we have been given the same power to create with our words. Proverbs 18:21 say that life and death are in the power of the tongue. God has a Soul (mind, will and emotions). His Mind is amazing, His Will is perfect and His emotions are always based on His Goodness and Righteousness, even in anger or judgment.

The following scriptures reveal the soul of God:

> Jeremiah 32:41
> 41 Yes, I will rejoice over them to do them good, and I will assuredly plant them in this land, with all My heart and with all My soul.'

> Hebrews 10:38
> 38 *Now the just shall live by faith; But if anyone draws back, My soul has no pleasure in him.*"

God lives in a glorified Body as seen when He appeared to Moses in Exodus 33:20–23 (NLT):

> 20 But you may not look directly at my face, for no one may see me and live." 21 The LORD continued, "Look, stand near me on this rock. 22 As my glorious presence passes by, I will hide you in the crevice of the rock and cover you with my hand until I have passed by. 23 Then I will remove my hand and let you see me from behind. But my face will not be seen."

Just like God we are a triune being – spirit, soul and body. When we receive Jesus as Savior and Lord of our lives, we are made a new creation (II Corinthians 5:17). Jesus lives in us enabling us by His Spirit to live the Christian life. Our spirit is perfect but our soul (mind, will and emotions) must be changed by making choices that line up with God's Word (Romans 12:2). Our will is important both to God and to us. He gave us a free will to be able to choose His way of doing and being right. Jesus said that those who obey me are those who love Me (John 14:15). Our will is the "seat of choice" that determines what choices we make for God. And, the choices we make for God affects all the people around us who are watching our lives. The third part of our triune being is the body, which the Word calls "God's temple." We must take good care of it and honor God with it (Romans 12:1). In our spirit, soul and body we are made in the image of our Heavenly Father. Psalm 139:14 sums it up: "I will praise You, for I am fearfully and wonderfully made in Your image and likeness."

As we get greater revelation of God as our "Abba" Father, scripture takes on greater meaning. Imagine the joy in our Heavenly Father's heart as He released Jesus into the earth to be born in the manger, knowing that it marked the beginning of bringing the family He always desired back into fellowship with Him. Yet, imagine thirty-three years later, the anguish Father God felt as He saw His Son being crucified, taking on the sin of the world so His relationship with Man could be restored. Imagine the agony the Father experienced each time He heard the hammer connect with the nails being driven into His Son's body. Yet Father God allowed it because of His unfailing love for mankind.

John 17:23 says that Father God loves us just as much as He loves Jesus. How can we fully grasp that fact? We need only to look to the Cross. The worth of an item is determined by how much one is willing to give to get the item he desires. What did our salvation cost Father God? It cost Him everything - the life of His Only Son. It was a priceless gift given by Love Himself! As a result, our loving Heavenly Father is free to lavish His Love on all who will receive it. I Timothy 6:17b reveals the Heart of our Heavenly Father when Timothy says we should put our trust in God … "Who richly *and* ceaselessly provides us with everything for [our] enjoyment."

So Great a Salvation

When Jesus Christ hung on the Cross the last words He cried out were, "It is finished"! With His Blood He paid for it all – all sin past, present and future! He took our place so He could enter into Hell to strip and defeat Satan by taking back the power and the authority that Satan had stolen from Adam and Eve in the Garden of Eden. The book of Revelation, Chapter 1:18 shows us the victory Jesus won over Satan:

> [18] I *am* He who lives, and was dead, and behold,
> I am alive forevermore. Amen. And I have the
> keys of Hades and of Death.

Colossians 2:13-15 describes in detail what the victory entailed:

> [13] And you, being dead in your trespasses and
> the uncircumcision of your flesh, He has made
> alive together with Him, having forgiven you all
> trespasses, [14] having wiped out the handwriting
> of requirements that was against us, which was

contrary to us. And He has taken it out of the way, having nailed it to the cross. [15] Having disarmed principalities and powers, He made a public spectacle of them, triumphing over them in it.

With the victory won, Jesus had one last act to complete. When He was raised to life Jesus appeared to Mary and told her not to touch Him because He had to first go to His Father in Heaven. There Jesus presented His Blood to cover the Mercy Seat. At that time the terms of the New Covenant were sworn between God the Father and Jesus His Son. Jesus was given all authority in Heaven and Earth (Matthew 28:18). He is the Heir of all! When we prayed a prayer to accept Jesus as Savior and Lord of our lives and confessed that God had raised Him from the dead, we were saved (Romans 10:9-10). At that time we became joint heirs together with Christ (Romans 8:17). Ephesians 2:4-6 tells us that God has raised us up together and made us to sit in the heavenly places in Christ Jesus, far above all principalities and powers. He has given us all authority over all demonic power and said nothing would harm us (Luke 10:19). According to Matthew 16:19 Jesus has given us the keys of the Kingdom of Heaven: Matthew 16:19 (AMP)

> [19] I will give you the keys of the kingdom of heaven; and whatever you bind (declare to be improper and unlawful) on earth must be what is already bound in heaven; and whatever you loose (declare lawful) on earth must be what is already loosed in heaven.

When we were born-again, we received many privileges that belong to the children of the King. We were made citizens of heaven and given the title of "ambassador" by the Lord. The definition of the word ambassador is a person who is a high-ranking diplomat who represents his country's affairs in another country. As citizens of heaven we are called to conduct our Father's business in this world. We do that by presenting His love and His forgiveness to a dark and dying world. II Corinthians 5:20 (AMP) states:

> [20] So we are Christ's ambassadors, God making His appeal as it were through us. We [as Christ's personal representatives] beg you for His sake to lay hold of the divine favor [now offered you] *and* be reconciled to God.

Not only do we share the Father's love as His ambassadors; we receive our needs met as His representatives. In the natural world, when an ambassador is sent to another country all of his provisions are provided for by the country he is representing – especially his protection while in a foreign land. Likewise, we can expect our Heavenly Father to meet our needs and protect us while we represent Him here on earth (Psalm 91:11 AMP).

The gift of salvation became available to us through Jesus' death and resurrection. The abundant life Jesus spoke of in John 10:10 is our inheritance as children of God. Jesus said He came to give us abundant life. In Vines Expository Dictionary of New Testament Words, it explains that the word for life is "zoe", which means "life as God has it." Jesus came to restore to us the freedom that Adam and Eve had when they walked and fellowshipped with God in the Garden of Eden. Jesus is referred to as the last Adam who brought us back to God and made every provision for us (I Corinthians 15:45). He is our salvation! The word "salvation" means so much more than going to heaven when we die. The Greek word for salvation is "soteria". It literally means deliverance from danger and apprehension, pardon, restoration, healing, wholeness and soundness.

I believe "wholeness in every area of our lives" is the best way to describe salvation. It is healing for your body, peace for your mind, and righteousness for your spirit. The term includes physical and spiritual protection, prosperity and financial blessing. It truly is the "salvation package" and God has taken care of every area of our lives. He is a good God Who takes very good care of us! The following scripture reminds us of His goodness:

> Psalm 68:19–20 (NLT)
> [19] Praise the Lord; praise God our savior! For each day he carries us in his arms. *Interlude* [20] Our God is a God who saves! The Sovereign LORD rescues us from death.

> Psalm 68:19–20 [19]Blessed *be* the Lord, *Who* daily loads us *with benefits,* The God of our salvation! Selah [20]Our God *is* the God of salvation; And to GOD the Lord *belong* escapes from death.

Some people might ask, "If all these benefits are supplied for me in salvation, why am I not experiencing them?" While all of these benefits belong to us when we become born again, they don't come automatically. They can only be manifested in our life as we trust God for each one. For example, when you received Jesus as Lord it was because you heard the Word about how to be saved and made a decision to receive that promise. Even though salvation was yours, you continued to get sick. Then you heard scriptures about healing such as Psalm 103:3 which says God heals all your diseases. You discovered I Peter 2:24 which says that by Jesus stripes you were healed. As you grew in the knowledge of what the Word promises in that specific area you began to walk in God's provision for healing. The pattern is the same for all the provisions included in salvation; you discover a provision, you believe you receive it, and then let the Word concerning the particular provision grow in your heart until it is a settled issue.

God has supplied all that we would ever need or desire through His grace (unmerited favor). Our response to His abundant supply is to receive what He has done by faith (Ephesians 2:8-9); which means to trust Him to do what He said He would do. The Word of God warns us in Hebrews 2:3 not to neglect so great a salvation. The definition for neglect is "to ignore, or disregard, or fail to attend to properly". We must rightly divide the Word of God and be a disciple of the Truth. We must put God and His Word first place in our lives. This is made very clear in Matthew 6:33 (AMP):

> [33] But seek (aim at and strive after) first of all His kingdom and His righteousness (His way of doing and being right), and then all these things taken together will be given you besides.

In Philippians 2:12-13 the apostle Paul is telling us we must be doers of God's Word:

> [12] Therefore, my beloved, as you have always obeyed, not as in my presence only, but now much more in my absence, work out your own salvation with fear and trembling; [13] for it is God who works in you both to will and to do for *His* good pleasure.

The Lord is telling us how very serious this is. We have an enemy, Satan, who comes to steal, kill, and destroy the abundant life God intends us to have (John 10:10). The Bible warns us in I Peter 5:8 to be alert to his devices:

> [8] Be sober, be vigilant; because your adversary the devil walks about like a roaring lion, seeking whom he may devour.

God wants us to be strong and courageous fighting the "good fight of faith." (I Timothy 6:12). All of His promises are "yea and amen" to those who believe (II Corinthians 1:20), but they can only be activated by our faith in God and in His Word. It is our faith that brings them to pass in our lives. God's promise is that He will always cause us to triumph (II Corinthians 2:14) when we truly trust Him with our lives.

In the first chapter of this book, God's Amazing Plan, we see the wonderful future we have in the Lord. In the Lord's Prayer Jesus makes it clear that salvation is to be enjoyed not only in eternity but also as we live out our lives here on the earth (Matthew 6:9–10):

> [9] In this manner, therefore, pray: Our Father in heaven, Hallowed be Your name. [10]Your kingdom come. Your will be done, On earth as *it is* in heaven.

When Jesus prayed that prayer He was looking to the Cross and what was to be accomplished there. As a result of His death, burial, resurrection and ascension, that prayer has been answered. His kingdom has come and with it "so great a salvation"; the only thing that remains is for us to walk in the fullness of it!

God's Perfect Protection

We are living in very dangerous times. I believe II Timothy 3:1–5 speaks of the days we are living in:

> ¹ But know this, that in the last days perilous times will come: ² For men will be lovers of themselves, lovers of money, boasters, proud, blasphemers, disobedient to parents, unthankful, unholy,³ unloving, unforgiving, slanderers, without self-control, brutal, despisers of good,⁴ traitors, headstrong, haughty, lovers of pleasure rather than lovers of God, ⁵ having a form of godliness but denying its power. And from such people turn away!

People are fearful and confused as they watch the news every night. They are asking questions like what are we going to do? Crime is rampant in our streets. Our economy is failing and our weather systems are unpredictable and increasingly destructive. Conditions internationally are continuing to deteriorate.

We are living in the last days and Jesus warned us about what to expect. In Matthew 24:37–39 He said,

> [37] But as the days of Noah *were,* so also will the coming of the Son of Man be. [38] For as in the days before the flood, they were eating and drinking, marrying and giving in marriage, until the day that Noah entered the ark, [39] and did not know until the flood came and took them all away, so also will the coming of the Son of Man be.

What was it like in the days of Noah? Genesis 6:11–12 (AMP) describes it:

> [11] The earth was depraved *and* putrid in God's sight, and the land was filled with violence (desecration, infringement, outrage, assault, and lust for power). [12] And God looked upon the world and saw how degenerate, debased, *and* vicious it was, for all humanity had corrupted their way upon the earth *and* lost their true direction.

The Word of God is very clear about the Lord wanting His people to be protected at all times. Psalm 4:8 says, "I will both lie down in peace, and sleep; For You alone, O LORD, make me dwell in safety." *New Living Translation* says it this way: "I will both lie down in peace and sleep. You alone Oh Lord keep me safe!" If ever there was a time to walk closely to the Lord, it's now! We don't have to fear. In fact, we are commanded by God not to fear (II Timothy 1:7)! If we put our trust in Him and stay close to Him, He will keep us safe and at peace in very hard times. Psalm 91 (AMP) outlines God's plan for our safety.

¹ He who dwells in the secret place of the Most High shall remain stable *and* fixed under the shadow of the Almighty [Whose power no foe can withstand].

² I will say of the Lord, He is my Refuge and my Fortress, my God; on Him I lean *and* rely, *and* in Him I [confidently] trust!

³ For [then] He will deliver you from the snare of the fowler and from the deadly pestilence.

⁴ [Then] He will cover you with His pinions, and under His wings shall you trust *and* find refuge; His truth *and* His faithfulness are a shield and a buckler.

⁵ You shall not be afraid of the terror of the night, nor of the arrow (the evil plots and slanders of the wicked) that flies by day,

⁶ Nor of the pestilence that stalks in darkness, nor of the destruction *and* sudden death that surprise *and* lay waste at noonday.

⁷ A thousand may fall at your side, and ten thousand at your right hand, but it shall not come near you.

⁸ Only a spectator shall you be [yourself inaccessible in the secret place of the Most High] as you witness the reward of the wicked.

⁹ Because you have made the Lord your refuge, and the Most High your dwelling place, [Ps. 91:1, 14.]

¹⁰ There shall no evil befall you, nor any plague *or* calamity come near your tent.

¹¹ For He will give His angels [especial] charge over you to accompany *and* defend *and* preserve you in all your ways [of obedience and service].

¹² They shall bear you up on their hands, lest you dash your foot against a stone. [Luke 4:10, 11; Heb. 1:14.]

¹³ You shall tread upon the lion and adder; the young lion and the serpent shall you trample underfoot. [Luke 10:19.]

¹⁴ Because he has set his love upon Me, therefore will I deliver him; I will set him on high, because he knows *and* understands My name [has a personal knowledge of My mercy, love, and kindness—trusts and relies on Me, knowing I will never forsake him, no, never].

¹⁵ He shall call upon Me, and I will answer him; I will be with him in trouble, I will deliver him and honor him.

¹⁶ With long life will I satisfy him and show him My salvation.

Psalm 91 has many parallels to Noah's situation. God told Noah to build an ark for safety for him and his family. I believe God is telling us to do the same thing today. Our ark is built by receiving the promises of protection in Psalm 91. While receiving the promises of protection for the foundation of our ark, there are other very important conditions for us to meet that are found in Psalm 91. Let's look at Psalm 91 verse by verse and find out what our part is. We will see that the first two verses tell us what our part is in receiving God's protection. Verses 2-15 tell us about God's commitment to protect and deliver us. As we receive the conditions and promises of Psalm 91 we will be able to trust God to do His part more easily.

Psalm 91:1 (AMP)
¹ *He who dwells in the secret place of the Most High shall remain stable and fixed under the shadow of the Almighty [Whose power no foe can withstand].*

The first condition we must meet is to abide in the secret place. It is not a place where you come and go. It is a permanent dwelling place; it is a place of continual fellowship with the Lord. You don't add the Lord to your life – He is your life! How do we become an "abider"? We must put the Word of God in our hearts. Jesus said in John 15:7 (AMP) "If you live in Me [abide vitally united to Me] and My words remain in you *and* continue to live in your hearts, ask whatever you will, and it shall be done for you."

Abiding under the shadow of the Almighty will happen as you spend time in His Word; as the Word becomes engrafted in your heart you will begin "practicing His Presence".

When disaster hits, you will automatically react in faith without even giving it a thought.

Abiding also includes being obedient. 1 John 3:6 (AMP) says,

[6] No one who abides in Him [who lives and remains in communion with and in obedience to Him—deliberately, knowingly, and habitually] commits (practices) sin. No one who [habitually] sins has either seen *or* known Him [recognized, perceived, or understood Him, or has had an experiential acquaintance with Him].

If you read the first chapter of Proverbs you will see just how dangerous disobedience can be. Disobedience can be one reason that when some people need protection from God it is not there for them. Proverbs 1:29-31 (AMP) says,

[29] Because they hated knowledge and did not choose the reverent *and* worshipful fear of the Lord,

[30] Would accept none of my counsel, and despised all my reproof,

[31] Therefore shall they eat of the fruit of their own way and be satiated with their own devices.

Thank God we're living in a day of mercy and grace and you can go to the Lord and repent (change). Proverbs 1:33 (AMP) tells us where we want to be: "But whoso hearkens to me [Wisdom] shall dwell securely *and* in confident trust and shall be quiet, without fear *or* dread of evil."

Psalm 91:2 (AMP)

[2] *I will say of the Lord, He is my Refuge and my Fortress, my God; on Him I lean and rely, and in Him I [confidently] trust!*

"I will say" … We must speak our faith. We say, "He is my refuge and fortress. I confidently trust in my God!" Trusting in our heart is not enough; we have to say it with our mouths in order to activate the promise in our lives. Faith has to be released in the natural realm by our words in order to bring God's supernatural power to us. Think of the difference it would make if when a crisis came, your dependence was on the Lord, rather than on the world and you declared that boldly from the onset of the challenge. That's why we have to become disciples (learners) of God's Word in order to be delivered – we cannot speak about something about which we have no knowledge.

Psalm 91:3 (AMP)

3For [then] He will deliver you from the snare of the fowler and from the deadly pestilence. 4 [Then] He will cover you with His pinions, and under His wings shall you trust and find refuge; His truth and His faithfulness are a shield and a buckler.

Because you have spoken out that God is your refuge and fortress, peace is released on the inside of you. Now you can be confident of supernatural protection on the outside. God promises us protection from the snare of the fowler (devil) and from pestilence. Snares are traps set by the devil in order to cause us harm. Pestilence are plagues; malignant, contagious or infectious epidemic diseases which are deadly and devastating. (Luke 21:11 AMP) Cancer and Aids seem to fall into this category. The Lord promises us in this passage that He will cover us with His pinions and under His wings we will find refuge. I picture a mother hen and her chicks; when danger comes the mother hen calls out to her chicks and they run to her and get under her wings for protection. The Bible says in I Peter 5:8 that the devil goes looking for those he can devour. I truly believe that he cannot find us when we are under our Father's wings!

Psalm 91:5-8 (AMP)

⁵ You shall not be afraid of the terror of the night, nor of the arrow (the evil plots and slanders of the wicked) that flies by day, ⁶ Nor of the pestilence that stalks in darkness, nor of the destruction and sudden death that surprise and lay waste at noonday. ⁷ A thousand may fall at your side, and ten thousand at your right hand, but it shall not come near you. ⁸ Only a spectator shall you be [yourself inaccessible in the secret place of the Most High] as you witness the reward of the wicked.

The promises in the verses 5-8 are definitely for today. We live in a day when thousands of people can be killed by chemical weapons or nuclear warfare that can destroy whole cities. Yet God promises us that even a thousand can fall at one side and ten thousand at the other but it won't come near us. Once again, we must receive these promises by faith. And we do that by confessing God's Word concerning protection. The following scriptures should be confessed often:

Psalm 5:11–12 (AMP)

¹¹ But let all those who take refuge *and* put their trust in You rejoice; let them ever sing *and* shout for joy, because You make a covering over them *and* defend them; let those also who love Your name be joyful in You *and* be in high spirits.

¹² For You, Lord, will bless the [uncompromisingly] righteous [him who is upright and in right standing with You]; as with a shield You will surround him with goodwill (pleasure and favor).

Psalm 27:5 (AMP)

⁵ For in the day of trouble He will hide me in His shelter; in the secret place of His tent will He hide me; He will set me high upon a rock.

The more we confess these scriptures and others that talk about protection, the more faith will arise within us (Romans 10:17).

Psalm 91:9–10 (AMP)

⁹ *Because you have made the Lord your refuge, and the Most High your dwelling place, [Ps. 91:1, 14.]* ¹⁰ *There shall no evil befall you, nor any plague or calamity come near your tent.*

Making the Lord our refuge comes by knowing and believing His promises. That, in turn, positions us to be protected from plagues and calamities.

Psalm 91:11–12 (AMP)

¹¹ *For He will give His angels [especial] charge over you to accompany and defend and preserve you in all your ways [of obedience and service].*

¹² *They shall bear you up on their hands, lest you dash your foot against a stone.*

One of the ways God protects and delivers us is through His angels. We've all seen art work showing baby angels floating around on clouds. Nothing could be further from the Truth! In Vine's Dictionary of New Testament Words, it says that angels are always spoken of in the masculine gender. They are spirits (Hebrews 1:14) that are mighty and powerful; they can assume a human form when necessary. According to the Bible, God has assigned an angel to every child who would become an heir of

His salvation. Psalm 103:20-21 we are told that angels come to our aid when we confess the Word of God. They watch over God's Word to perform it; angels are powerful and mighty, always poised to defend us.

The Bible says that we can entertain angels unaware (Hebrews 13:2). My husband Ernie and I have experienced this. We were on our way to church on the interstate on a Wednesday night traveling seventy miles an hour. We had a tire blow out and were being tossed about while Ernie brought the car to a stop. As we pulled onto the side of the road we noticed that there was an unmarked truck pulled over near where we stopped. A man came running from the truck to see if we were okay. He insisted on changing our tire. When he finished Ernie offered him ten dollars and he smiled and said so sweetly, "No, thank you – you just say a prayer for me." Then he left. There was something so loving and heavenly about him that we knew God had given us favor and supplied for us even before we knew we had a need.

Another time I was in a grocery store making a quick stop to pick up something. As I was hurrying down the aisle I noticed a very unusual-looking elderly woman who was very old and feeble looking just shuffling along. She had on a hat and house slippers. She stopped me and asked if I knew where two items were located. I went over a couple of aisles and brought back one of the items to her. She talked in such a soft voice that you could hardly hear her. But when she saw that I had the item she wanted, she smiled and with a booming voice said, "Your reward is in Heaven." I thought, wow! I then went looking for the other item that she needed. I found it within about a minute and returned to find her no longer in the aisle. I went up and down all the aisles; there was no way she could have left the store in that short period of time because of the way she had trouble walking. Then I felt the Holy Spirit, and I knew I had entertained an angel of God. I can't tell you how much these experienced have blessed my life. Some people have a hard time believing in angels but I know they are a part of my life on a daily basis.

Psalm 91:13 (AMP)

[13] *You shall tread upon the lion and adder; the young lion and the serpent shall you trample underfoot.*

In Luke 10:19 Jesus said He has given us all authority over all demonic power and that nothing would harm us. He has also provided the armor of God (which is the Word of God) for victory over Satan and His forces in every area of our lives. Hebrews 4:12 tells us that God's Word is living and powerful. The armor of God provides protection for every area of our lives:

> [10] Finally, my brethren, be strong in the Lord and in the power of His might. [11] Put on the whole armor of God, that you may be able to stand against the wiles of the devil. [12] For we do not wrestle against flesh and blood, but against principalities, against powers, against the rulers of the darkness of this age, against spiritual *hosts* of wickedness in the heavenly *places.* [13] Therefore take up the whole armor of God, that you may be able to withstand in the evil day, and having done all, to stand.
>
> [14] Stand therefore, having girded your waist with truth, having put on the breastplate of righteousness, [15] and having shod your feet with the preparation of the gospel of peace; [16] above all, taking the shield of faith with which you will be able to quench all the fiery darts of the wicked one. [17] And take the helmet of salvation, and the sword of the Spirit, which is the word of God; [18] praying always with all prayer and supplication

in the Spirit, being watchful to this end with all perseverance and supplication for all the saints—
Ephesians 6:10–18

The Word instructs us to take authority over evil. This is especially important in the day in which we live. Coupled with taking authority over evil we must also honor God in all we do. In the book of Malachi the people of that time did not honor God. They were always complaining to Him and said things like "it is useless to serve God." But the people of God showed Him honor and it pleased God so much that He made a book of remembrance. In Malachi 3:17 God shows us how he will protect those who honor Him and hold Him in reverence:

> [17] And they shall be mine, saith the LORD of hosts,
> In that day when I make up my jewels; And I will spare them, as a man spareth his own son that serveth him.

In Malachi 4:1-3 God tells us that the wicked will be utterly destroyed in the Tribulation but those who honor and reverence Him will triumph in the last days:

> [1]For, behold, the day cometh, that shall burn as an oven; And all the proud, yea, and all that do wickedly, shall be stubble:
> And the day that cometh shall burn them up, saith the LORD of hosts,
> That it shall leave them neither root nor branch.
> [2]But unto you that fear my name shall the Sun of righteousness arise
> With healing in his wings;
> And ye shall go forth, and grow up as calves of the stall.

³And ye shall tread down the wicked;
For they shall be ashes under the soles of your feet
In the day that I shall do *this*, saith the LORD of
hosts.

Notice verse 3 says that we shall trample the wicked, for they shall be ashes under our feet. That is the assurance from the Lord that we will be protected and victorious over our enemy.

Psalm 91:14-16 (AMP)

¹⁴ *Because he has set his love upon Me, therefore will I deliver him; I will set him on high, because he knows and understands My name [has a personal knowledge of My mercy, love, and kindness—trusts and relies on Me, knowing I will never forsake him, no, never].* ¹⁵ *He shall call upon Me, and I will answer him; I will be with him in trouble, I will deliver him and honor him.* ¹⁶ *With long life will I satisfy him and show him My salvation.*

The first word of this passage, "Because", is very important. By setting our love upon the Lord, we are saying that He is number one in our lives. Because He is number one in our lives it is easy for us to believe that He will see us through times of trouble victoriously. God will set us on high, meaning He will honor us because we know the meaning of His Name. He is the great "I AM". He is my Savior, my healer, my provider and my deliverer. He is everything to me. He is my very life! Father God wants me to be satisfied with a long life. In a word, He is my Salvation!

Once we start trusting God to protect and defend us in every situation, we will position ourselves to start hearing directions and admonitions from the Holy Spirit. They will not always seem very spiritual. Part of God's supernatural protection can come as a warning. You may be getting ready to go to the grocery and the thought comes to your mind, "Don't go to the grocery store the way you usually go. Take a different road." Or maybe you will sense that you shouldn't go to the grocery store at all. In either instance it could be the Holy Spirit trying to protect you from an accident or perhaps a robbery that would take place at that store. Remember in Psalm 91:3 it says that He will deliver you from the snares (traps) of the fowler (devil).

We see in Matthew 2:12 how God warned the wise men in a dream not to return to Herod. In verse 13 an angel appeared to Joseph and gave him instructions that would protect His family:

> [12] Now when they had departed, behold, an angel of the Lord appeared to Joseph in a dream, saying, "Arise, take the young Child and His mother, flee to Egypt, and stay there until I bring you word; for Herod will seek the young Child to destroy Him."

You can see how God uses the angels so much in our lives. They are with us everywhere we go! The Word says, "The Angel of the Lord encamps around those who fear God." (Psalm 34:7)

We had an experience like this one time. We had gone to Michigan to visit family. On our way home we stopped at a motel; after settling in we went out for dinner. When we returned to our room I kept being drawn to put the chain lock on the door, which normally I would not have done until we went to bed. But the thought persisted that I should put the chain on immediately. So I did. At 2:00 am we were awakened by a very loud bang. Someone must have put a key in our lock and when they tried to open the door, the chain lock stopped them. When they realized they couldn't break it they ran away. If I hadn't put the chain lock in place when the Lord told me to, anything could have happened to us that night.

God has made every provision for our deliverance and protection but we must do our part by believing and receiving

Him as our refuge and fortress and trusting Him with all our heart! The key to being able to have that kind of confidence is found is Psalm 91:14 (AMP):

> 14 Because he has set his love upon Me, therefore will I deliver him; I will set him on high, because he knows *and* understands My name [has a personal knowledge of My mercy, love, and kindness—trusts and relies on Me, knowing I will never forsake him, no, never].

God wants you to understand His Name because when you get a revelation of His Name you get a personal knowledge of His Mercy, Love, Kindness and Grace. That knowledge gives you the confident expectation that you can trust and rely on Him in any situation, no matter how threatening or dangerous. When you are walking with the King, you are walking in a place of protection where all attacks of the enemy have been denied their power to harm you (John 16:33 AMP)!

The Leading of the Holy Spirit

The leading of the Holy Spirit will be very important to us in the last days! He needs to guide us through these very dangerous times. Jesus, speaking in John 14:15-17,26 (AMP) is showing us the role of the Holy Spirit in our lives:

> [15] If you [really] love Me, you will keep (obey) My commands. [16] And I will ask the Father, and He will give you another Comforter (Counselor, Helper, Intercessor, Advocate, Strengthener, and Standby), that He may remain with you forever— [17] The Spirit of Truth, Whom the world cannot receive (welcome, take to its heart), because it does not see Him or know *and* recognize Him. But you know *and* recognize Him, for He lives with you [constantly] and will be in you.)
>
> [26] But the Comforter (Counselor, Helper, Intercessor, Advocate, Strengthener, Standby), the Holy Spirit, Whom the Father will send in My name [in My place, to represent Me and act on

My behalf], He will teach you all things. And He will cause you to recall (will remind you of, bring to your remembrance) everything I have told you.

Once you have revelation of the Holy Spirit's role in your life and begin walking in faith for your protection you will start hearing some direction or promptings from the Spirit of God. No matter how simple these instructions sound, you must pay close attention to them. The Holy Spirit will always show you things to come with warning and direction as He guides you every day. The Bible tells us that in the days ahead we will see an increase of trouble in the world around us. Things on this earth are going to get worse, just like they did in Noah's day. While the darkness will increase, the believer's life will grow brighter and brighter as we extend our faith and expect Jesus to come at any moment.

We need to learn a lesson from Noah. That lesson is that we should not wait until trouble comes to start building our ark; we want to have it finished before trouble comes. Just think about how Noah was laughed at and ridiculed. The people around him probably called him crazy as they watched him building a ship on dry ground. Water was no where to be seen at the time. Rain had yet to fall (the earth was covered by a continual mist). The idea of a flood was something the people could not comprehend. The Word says that during the time that Noah and his sons were building the ark people had no idea of the dangers ahead. Only on the day the rain began to fall did they realize they were in danger and by then it was too late; they were swept away. But Noah believed and obeyed God and knew exactly what God was going to do. As a result he and his family were prepared. So we, too, must build our ark of safety in advance of Jesus' appearing.

The Bible says that God speaks in a small, still voice. The enemy is always loud and drives you to make a decision or to act in a hurry; it is always "now or never" with him. God, however, leads us by His peace. He expects us to look for His leading in all situations. If we will heed the Words of Proverbs 3:5-6, we will be safe:

> ⁵Trust in the LORD with all your heart,
> And lean not on your own understanding;
> ⁶In all your ways acknowledge Him,
> And He shall direct your paths.

When the first sign of trouble appears you need to immediately bind fear in the name of Jesus. You need to pay close attention to your inner impressions and thoughts and the Holy Spirit will direct you on what to do. You must be ready to change your plans if the Spirit of God is directing you to do so. It could save your life! Psalm 91:3 says that the Lord will deliver us from the traps of the devil.

Often believers will say they cannot hear from God. But according to John 10:2,3,14 (NLT) every believer can hear from God:

> ² But the one who enters through the gate is the shepherd of the sheep.
> ³ The gatekeeper opens the gate for him, and the sheep recognize his voice and come to him. He calls his own sheep by name and leads them out.
> ¹⁴ "I am the good shepherd; I know my own sheep, and they know me,

The first thing that has to happen before you can begin to hear from God is that you must know and believe what the Word says about hearing from Him. You must begin to think and confess that you always hear what God is saying (you start this before you have heard a word!) Next you must realize that when the Lord speaks to us it is usually not in an audible voice. That does happen but usually not on a regular basis. Most of the time a person experiences a knowing on the inside that wells up out of his spirit. That is called an inward witness. Much like a natural relationship grows and develops as you spend time with another person, so your relationship with the Holy Spirit likewise matures as you fellowship with Him through prayer and meditating on His Word. In the natural you know the voice of someone you are close to; the same is true for the Holy Spirit. Knowing the voice of the Holy Spirit and His leading is very important so you won't be deceived by the voice of the enemy.

When we receive direction from the Lord it will bring peace. This peace is an indicator that you are moving in the right direction. Don't do anything about your situation until you experience that inner peace.

Colossians 3:15 (AMP) says,
¹⁵ And let the peace (soul harmony which comes) from Christ rule (act as umpire continually) in your hearts [deciding and settling with finality all questions that arise in your minds, in that peaceful state] to which as [members of Christ's] one body you were also called [to live]. And be thankful (appreciative), [giving praise to God always].

I've heard several incidents where people were planning to leave on a trip and God told them to go a different way or told them to wait a while before leaving. People were told not to board an airplane and later that flight crashed. In spite of having that inner peace, you must remember that the devil may try to fill you with fear when you are getting on a plane. In that case you simply cast down that fear in the Name of Jesus and board the plane in God's peace.

The key to receiving the Holy Spirit's direction in all matters is to desire to hear His voice and to be willing to take the time to learn to recognize His voice. When the 9-11 tragedy happened in New York in 2001, there were so many testimonies of how the Lord delayed people from being on time for their jobs in the World Trade Center. There was one particular testimony that really moved me. When the plane hit the first tower, a Christian woman was in the second tower sitting at her desk. An announcement came over the loud speakers telling people in the second tower that they should remain in the building and not panic. Immediately this woman had a strong impression to, "Get out of here and take as many people with you as possible." She followed His instructions and as they were running down the stairs the other plane slammed into the floor where she had been. This woman and those who heeded her cry to get out of the building were safe because she knew how to hear from the Holy Spirit. There have been questions about why so many Christians lost their lives on that day. A very well-known evangelist asked the Lord about it and immediately had this thought, "I warned every one of them, but many did not hear me."

There are people who love God and who are truly born-again but never go on to develop a close walk with Him. They go to church but don't spend time with Him to learn His Word. As a result, many of them experience disastrous things in their lives. Hearing God's voice doesn't come automatically. You must spend time with Him every day to know His ways and to recognize His voice for direction. Hosea 4:6a shows us the importance of knowing His Word: "My people are destroyed for lack of knowledge ..." Without knowing and doing what God says to do opens the door for the devil to get an inroad into our lives.

The devil is always looking for an entrance into a believer's life. Jesus warns us in John 10:10 that the devil is a stealer, a killer and a destroyer. 1 Peter 5:8 warns us to constantly be aware of his method of operation: "Be sober, be vigilant; because your adversary the devil walks about like a roaring lion, seeking whom he may devour." He is a defeated foe, but that doesn't stop him. We must enforce his defeat by standing firm on the promises of

God. Jesus' sacrifice two thousand years ago not only defeated the devil but also bought for us a redemption that in effect put us spiritually back in the Garden of Eden before the fall. It was there that Adam and Eve fellowshipped with God and walked with him in the cool of the day. Today, once again, it is God's greatest joy to have His children's lives so transformed by His Love, His Mercy and His Grace that their greatest desire is to spend each day **walking with the King**!

Honoring God

God deserves all of our honor and respect for two reasons. First and most importantly He deserves our honor because of Who He is. There is none higher than Jehovah Elohim! That Hebrew name encompasses all that Father God is; He is Creator of all things, He is sovereign without exception and His authority is without question. Those factors alone require us to honor God. Yet there is another reason God deserves our honor. It is because of what He has done for us. God's love for man was such that when sin made it impossible for Him to fellowship with His beloved creation, God sent His very best to redeem mankind. His Son, Jesus, the One nearest and dearest to His heart, was sent to take away all of your sin and to suffer the punishment that was due you because of Adam and Eve's transgression in the Garden of Eden. In order for you to live eternally with your Heavenly Father, Jesus had to be obedient to His Father's plan of love for the redemption of mankind. That plan required Jesus to die by taking the sin of the world on Himself even though He Himself had never sinned (John 3:16). The Bible says that Jesus endured the cross for the "joy" that was set before Him (Hebrews 12:2). What could have enabled Jesus to endure the suffering He did? His love for His Father and His love for you is what Jesus focused on as He hung on that Cross. His desire was to see mankind restored to the original relationship that God had intended when He created man.

Jesus understood something that many people have yet to realize – that God loves each of us just as much as He loves Jesus (John 17:22-23). What an awesome statement! How could the Father have watched His only beloved Son being beaten, spat upon and having nails driven into His hands and feet? He, too, was looking beyond the Cross to the love He had for those who were separated from Him. Restoration could only be achieved by a divine sacrifice. Jesus paid the price and now the only thing that remains is for man to receive the benefits of that divine sacrifice.

When Jesus saved us, we became part of His Body, the Church. While many look at that description as something more figurative than literal, nothing could be further from the truth. Our part as His Body is to do the work Jesus did while He was on earth. For this reason, Jesus said that people should count the cost before making a commitment to Him (Luke 14:27-29, Matthew 16:24-27). He said it would require obedience, because the things He asks are not always easy. As we follow His Word we are confident that we are doing what He has called us to do (John 14:21). Our obedience to His Word is confirmation of our love for Him (I John 2:4-5). It is in our obedience that we honor God to the highest extent. How important is honor to God? He tells us in I Samuel 2:30: ... for those who honor Me I will honor, and those who despise (do not esteem) Me shall be lightly esteemed.

Yet, many in the Church today are not being obedient to His Word and, as a result are dishonoring God. Their commitment to the Lord goes only as far as attending a church service once or twice a week. When Jesus was being crucified, the very people whom He was sent to redeem cried out, "Kill Him!" Their guilt was in failing to recognize who He was and why He came into their lives. Our guilt is in failing to honor Him by being obedient to His Word and in failing to recognize that He needs us to complete His work here on the earth until He returns. When we fail to reach out to others we are holding back the work of God. We cannot treat the things of God carelessly. We are living in the last days. God has a plan for each of our lives (Jeremiah 29:11), and whatever the plan is we must do it quickly. Time is running out! He said He was coming back for a glorious Church without spot or wrinkle (Ephesians 5:25-27). We need to cooperate with the Holy Spirit in order to be a part of this great church that is ready for His return.

The book of Revelation describes two churches that represent the two different types of churches that exist in today's society – the Philadelphia church and the church of Laodicea. The Philadelphia church (Revelation 3:7-13) is very alive in the things of God and totally sold out to Jesus through obedience to Him and His Word. Jesus is very pleased with these believers and because He was first-place in their lives, He made a promise to them in verse ten: "Because you have kept my command to persevere, I also will keep you from the hour of trial which shall come upon the whole world to test those who dwell on the earth." He goes on to say in verse twelve that He will make these believers to be pillars in God's temple and that they will live in the New Jerusalem that comes down from heaven to the earth at the close of His thousand-year reign (also referred to in Revelation 21:2).

The Laodicean church (Revelation 3:14-22) was made up of people who were lukewarm believers. These people had made Jesus their Savior, but not the Lord of their lives. They were very lazy and disobedient when it came to serving God. They put other things before serving Him. As long as they had what they needed they gave no thought to their relationship with God. Helping others was not a priority in their lives. They were content to sit in their pews every week with a form of godliness but denying His power (II Timothy 3:4-5). This church was very upsetting to the Lord. He was sickened by their lukewarm attitude and said if they did not change, He would "vomit" them up, meaning they would have no part in Him.

What upset Jesus then and what upsets Him today is when He sees His Body unwilling to walk in the fullness of the life that He died to give us. We fail to honor, respect and be grateful for His sacrifice when we fail to obey His Word. He has provided everything we will ever need to live an abundant life (John 10:10). He died to give us "all things that pertain to life and godliness" (II Peter 1:3). He has given us His Blood (Covenant), His Word (promises) His Name (authority) and His weapons (mighty to the pulling down of strongholds) to enforce the defeat of the enemy. Although we face challenges to this abundant life continually because of the devil, the sin nature of this world, and our own undisciplined flesh, Jesus expects us to be overcomers. There is no excuse for not overcoming Satan if we listen to the Master (Luke 10:19).

Failure to obey God has consequences. The Old Testament gives us examples of what happens when people fail to obey God. As we look at these, remember that God is never out to "get" anyone. What happened then and what happens today comes about because disobedience removes us from the protective umbrella God wants over our lives. God doesn't do the moving; we do, when we are disobedient to His Word. In the book of Malachi, we can see the things that the people in Malachi's time did that displeased God and learn from them.

1. These people treated the things of God carelessly. They did not do what He had told them to do. They dishonored Him by saying that it was unimportant to them (Malachi 1:6-8).

2. The people gave the Lord meaningless offerings. What they gave to Him meant very little to them. They gave their "leftovers" – what they did not want. They gave but there was no honor in their giving, because their hearts were very far from Him.

3. There was no joy in the people's service to God. They felt that serving God was drudgery. They walked as mourners with a

"poor old me" attitude. They were so unthankful for all the things God had done for them (Malachi 3:14).

4. The leaders departed from God's Word, and they caused many who followed them to stumble (Malachi 2:7-8). They were not being taught about how great and loving God is and, as a result, bought the lie of Satan that God was causing all of their problems. The character of God was being maligned.

5. The people were always crying at the altar of God about the things they did wrong, but were unwilling to change (Malachi 2:13).

6. These people treated their spouses improperly. God hates divorce (Malachi 2:16) because it hurts so many lives. God expects His people to come to Him in order to work out the difficulties that occur in marriage. There are times when divorce does result even when people come to the Lord, because one or both parties involved choose not to obey God's Word. God does forgive divorce if those involved come to Him with true repentance.

7. People were saying evil is good and good is evil (Malachi 2:17). This is happening today in our society. Often it is coming from within the Church! We are to agree with what God says is evil and with what He says is good. God says homosexuality and abortion are wrong, but our society is accepting both practices more and more with each passing day.

8. The people were jealous of the wicked (Malachi 3:14,15). Their attitude was, "Why should we serve God; what good does it do? The wicked enjoy themselves and they go unpunished. We have to give up so much and they don't. Where's the reward in serving God?" What they failed to realize then and what many people fail to realize today is that often "successful" people are very unhappy with the lives they are living. The Bible says that there is pleasure in sin for a season (Hebrews 11:25). The Bible also says there is a price to pay for sin and that price is death. The so-called good times found in sin will eventually result in death (Romans 6:23).

9. The people robbed God of tithes and offerings (Malachi 3:6-10). This one is a very serious situation and is probably the root of many people's difficulties today in serving the Lord with joy. Jesus said that where your treasure is, there also is your heart (Matthew 6:21). A person cannot serve God and also serve money. The attitude then as well as today is, "I can't afford to pay my tithes". What that attitude fails to understand is that the blessings of God being poured out on God's people is directly connected to His people's willingness to be obedient in releasing their tithes to Him. Malachi makes perfectly clear that for those who obey and tithe, the windows of heaven will be opened and blessings that cannot be contained will be poured out on them. Blessing means to prosper in something desirable (spirit, soul and body). He also promises to rebuke the devourer (devil) for their sakes (Malachi 3:10-11). When Satan attacks, the Lord will rebuke him. For those who don't obey, a warning is given – a curse will be on their lives (Malachi 3:8-9). "Curse" doesn't mean that something terrible is going to happen to those who don't tithe. God is all good. But, "curse" means being separated from the blessings of God and being apart from His protective Hand.

The root of the problem in Malachi's day and also in society today is a lack of respect or lack of honor for God. In any relationship the most important element is respect. Proverbs 9:10 states, "The fear of the Lord is the beginning of wisdom". "Fear" in this verse means to respect, to hold in awe. We show our respect for God listening to His voice (that inner knowing) and doing those things He has told us to do in His Word. It not only pleases Him but allows Him to help protect us from the attacks of the enemy. Obedience to what God wants for our lives is a must. A life of obedience will have the Holy Spirit in charge. The degree to which you spend time with Him, listening to Him and obeying His Word, will determine our preparedness to meet Jesus when He returns for His glorious Church.

Matthew 25:1-13 is the parable of the ten virgins. This paints a picture of the condition of the end-time church. The virgins, whose lamps were filled, represent the Philadelphia church which is ready for the Lord's return. The virgins, who were caught with their lanterns empty, represent the Laodicean church that will be left behind to go through the tribulation. A closer look at these churches makes the distinction between the two very clear:

Philadelphia Church:
1. obedient to Jesus (doers of the Word)
2. on fire for God
3. dependent on the Holy Spirit for power in their lives
4. excited about/looked for Jesus' return

Laodicean Church:
1. disobedient (hearers only)
2. lazy and lukewarm
3. grieved the Holy Spirit by not relying on Him
4. didn't know enough about God's Word to be looking for His return

In another parable, the parable of the talents (Matthew 25:14-30), Jesus shows us how it will be at His coming. This parable has to do with being a good steward of what God has entrusted to us. Good stewards are obedient to God because of their love for Him. How a person spends his money reveals much about him. By looking at his checkbook, it would be clear where his heart is. If there were checks written for tithes and offerings, one would know that he loved God and was interested in helping carry out God's purposes for the world. The parable of the talents teaches us that if a person is faithful in what God calls him to do, God will give us more.

A person's love and loyalty to the Lord will determine to what extent he will be used by God. Without revelation of God's great love for you, you will see Him as religion sees Him – a hard taskmaster whom you can never really understand and never really please. The servant who hid his talents out of fear of God was like people today who never push beyond religious traditions to get to know God as He really is – a loving, compassionate, merciful God Who has a great plan for every individual life (Jeremiah 29:11). Jesus' words to this type of person were harsh as revealed in Matthew 25:30. In a parable He stated (concerning the person who had not used his talents wisely), " …cast this unprofitable servant into outer darkness. There will be weeping and gnashing of teeth." This kind of person is the one who is portrayed in the Laodicean church; he will be "vomited" up and left behind to go through the tribulation (Revelation 3:16). The good and faithful servant referred to in this parable, who did much with what the Lord had given him. He represents the Philadelphia church which will be raptured out by the Lord before the Tribulation begins (Revelation 3:10).

The third parable that deals with the return of Jesus for His Overcoming Church is found in Matthew 24:42-51. This parable gives us another picture of the wise and evil servants. The wise servant was looking for Jesus' return and the evil servant doubted His soon return (v. 48). This servant ("servant" indicates he was a part of the church) was the one who, because of his lukewarm, passive attitude, hindered the work of the church and lived like the world (v.49). When the master returned, he gave the evil servant his portion along with the rest of the wicked world (v. 51), which is the tribulation.

As believers we have a choice to make. Which "servant" will we be like? Jesus saves us, but what we do once that happens is entirely up to us. Either our love for the Lord will lead us on (by the power of the Holy Spirit) to be like the good and faithful servant, or we can refuse to change, and we will experience the wrath that God intended for the devil and his crowd during the tribulation. There are two gates before you. One gate leads to the world's way of living. It is very wide and ultimately leads to death. The other gate is very narrow, and it leads to God's way of living. It always leads to abundant life, both now and eternally (Matthew 7:13-14). Jesus stands before these gates wanting you to make the right choice, but He waits for you to make that decision. He will not make it for you. Once you make that choice, however, He stands ready to carry you through to His resurrection life. Why would anyone choose the gate that leads to death? Satan shows a person all the glitter of the world that appeals to the eyes of the flesh. He takes him further and further into the kingdom of darkness, and then, before the person knows it, Satan slams the door shut. All too suddenly the very thing that seemed to bring freedom now brings bondage. That's the reason Jesus came and gave His life for you – so you could come out of any darkness that encompasses you and make choices based on His Word. That Word will always result in a life that is worth living.

As we close this chapter I would like to go through a checklist that will assure you of being that good and faithful servant God has called you to be:

1. Put God and His Word first place in your life.
2. Show Him love by spending time praising and worshiping Him and by obeying Him
(through His Word).
3. Give the Holy Spirit total control of your life by spending time in His presence everyday.
4. Pay your tithes faithfully and give offerings to further His Kingdom on this earth.
5. Let your life show the Love of God; be "soul-minded", always ready to support God's work to win souls.
6. Always believe that God has your best interest in mind.
7. Always be grateful that He has chosen you to be His child.
8. Be thankful for all His provision and all of His goodness!

God is a Great Big Wonderful God who never changes! He will lead you to rule and reign with His Son, King Jesus, as He sets up His Kingdom on this earth for a thousand year reign. There will be peace like no other time in history. Finally, after the millennium is concluded, our Heavenly Father will come to live with us as the Heavenly New Jerusalem descends to earth. There we will live with Him and Jesus eternally. Those of us who have shown our love for Him by being obedient to His Word will be able to say what Paul said in II Timothy 4:7-8:

> [7] **"I have fought the good fight, I have finished the race. I have kept the faith.** [8] **Finally, there is laid up for me the crown of righteousness, which the Lord, the Righteous Judge, will give to me on that Day, and not to me only but also to all who have loved His appearing.**

Following Jesus Our King

I n order to follow Jesus closely we must always keep a childlike faith. Jesus said in Matthew 18:3 (AMP):

> ³ Truly I say to you, unless you repent (change, turn about) and become like little children [trusting, lowly, loving, forgiving], you can never enter the kingdom of heaven [at all].

Think for a moment what distinguishes a child from an adult (other than the obvious differences in age and size). The primary difference is the way in which a child responds to the cares of life. For the most part, a child has no cares. And on those occasions when he has a concern, the child immediately runs to his father, knowing he will take care of the problem. Who but a child can one minute be crying in his father's arms about a situation, and the next minute be running off with a big smile on his face to play, crisis resolved? In short, a child knows where to get his needs met. A child looks to his father with absolute trust in his ability to handle any problem, to fulfill any promise.

God's Word also refers to believers as sheep. Sheep are much like children when it comes to their relationship with the shepherd. The most noticeable characteristic of sheep is their total reliance on the shepherd. Sheep are so "in touch" with their shepherd that they respond to the sound of his voice. God has given believers the Holy Spirit as "His Voice" to which we can respond. When we learn to respond to that "inner witness" as readily as sheep respond to the voice of their shepherd, we will begin to see our needs and wants met with little effort on our part.

Psalm 23 (AMP) is a beautiful picture of a person who is living a victorious life following close to Jesus, His Shepherd. In this Psalm we see the seven redemptive names of the Lord.

Verse 1: "The Lord is my Shepherd (Jehovah-rohi) [to feed, guide, and shield me], I shall not lack. Philippians 4:19 (AMP) says, "And my God (Jehovah jirah) will liberally supply (fill to the full) your every need according to His riches in glory in Christ Jesus."

Verse 2: "He makes me lie down in [fresh, tender] green pastures; He leads me beside the still *and* restful waters." Jesus is the Prince of Peace (Jehovah-shalom); Isaiah 9:6. Jesus said in John 14:27 (AMP) "Peace I leave with you; My [own] peace I now give *and* bequeath to you. Not as the world gives do I give to you. Do not let your hearts be troubled, neither let them be afraid. [Stop allowing yourselves to be agitated and disturbed; and do not permit yourselves to be fearful and intimidated and cowardly and unsettled.]"

Verse 3: "He refreshes *and* restores (He is my healer, Jehovah-rophe) my life (myself)". Jesus took our infirmities and our sickness (Matthew 8:17). By His stripes we are healed (Isaiah 53:5, I Peter 2:24). He leads me in the paths of righteousness (Jehovah-tsidkenu) [uprightness and right standing with Him—not for my earning it, but] for His name's sake. Jesus is our guide. Psalm 37:23 (AMP) says, "The steps of a [good] man are directed *and* established by the Lord when He delights in his way [and He busies Himself with his every step]."

Verse 4: "Yea, though I walk through the [deep, sunless] valley of the shadow of death, I will fear *or* dread no evil, for You are with me (Jehovah-shammah – our ever-present God); Your rod (Your Word) [to protect] and Your staff (Holy Spirit) [to guide], they comfort me." Hebrews 13:5 (AMP) says " ...for He [God] Himself has said, I will not in any way fail you *nor* give you up *nor* leave you without support. [I will] not, [I will] not, [I will] not in any degree leave you helpless *nor* forsake *nor* let [you] down (relax My hold on you)! [Assuredly not!]" When we *believe* that Jesus has hold of our lives like this, we can make it through the darkest hours of any storm.

Verse 5: You prepare a table before me in the presence of my enemies (Jehovah-nissi; our God whose banner over us is love)." We always triumph in Christ (II Corinthians 2:14) "You anoint my head with oil; my [brimming] cup runs over." God has given us His armor to defeat our enemies. Ephesians 6:10-11 (AMP) says, "In conclusion, be strong in the Lord [be empowered through your union with Him]; draw your strength from Him [that strength which His boundless might provides]. 11 Put on God's whole armor [the armor of a heavy-armed soldier which God supplies], that you may be able successfully to stand up against [all] the strategies *and* the deceits of the devil. "God has also given us His Holy Spirit to empower us. Jesus said in Acts 1:8 (AMP) "But you shall receive power (ability, efficiency, and might) when the Holy Spirit has come upon you, and you shall be My witnesses in Jerusalem and all Judea and Samaria and to the ends (the very bounds) of the earth."

Verse 6: "Surely *or* only goodness, mercy, *and* unfailing love shall follow me all the days of my life, and through the length of my days the house of the Lord [and His presence] shall be my dwelling place."

This is God's perfect will for every one of his children – total trust and reliance on Him for every need to be met. When this happens a life full of joy and victory becomes possible. Psalm 16:11 (AMP) says, "You will show me the path of life; in Your presence is fullness of joy, at Your right hand there are pleasures forevermore."

The behavior of both children and sheep brings to mind two essential elements that believers must have in their walk with the Lord in order to enjoy the fullness of His blessings – trust and dependence. Psalm 91:2 (AMP) says, "I will say of the Lord, He is my Refuge and my Fortress, my God; on Him I lean *and* rely, *and* in Him I [confidently] trust!" God's love is available to all men, but His blessings are poured out in abundance only on those who choose to **follow Him closely and take Him at His Word!**

A Firm Foundation

What I have shared in this book has been my ongoing journey as a Christian who is maturing in the love God has for me. It is a journey that continues to take me from one revelation to another; with each one leading me to a deeper understanding of God's love toward His children. I have found that the reality of God's love for me is directly proportional to the liberation I enjoy today in my relationship with Him. I realize that many of the people who read this book will have already been born-again, and like me, are searching for more in their relationship with the Lord. But I also know that there will be many who read this book who will want to receive Christ as Savior and Lord of their lives who have not done so before.

How to Become a Christian

If you have never made Jesus the Lord of your life, then you are separated from God by sin. You are the reason that God sent Jesus to the cross – to pay the price for your sin, so you would not have to. John 3:16 says,

¹⁶ For God so loved the world that He gave His only begotten Son that whoever believes in Him should not perish but have everlasting life.

God loves you *that much* that He gave His very best for you! The Bible states very clearly in Romans 10:9,10 what we must do to become born of God (born-again or saved):

> ⁹ that if you confess with your mouth the Lord Jesus and believe in your heart that God raised Him from the dead, you will be saved. ¹⁰ For with the heart one believes unto righteousness, and with the mouth confession is made unto salvation.

I would like to pray with you now to receive Jesus. Just repeat this out loud:

> *Heavenly Father, I come to You in the name of Your Son, Jesus Christ. I now repent of all my sin. I pray that Jesus would be the Lord over my life. I believe that You raised Him from the dead. Jesus, please come into my heart and save me. Thank You. I now believe that I am a Christian and I will serve You all the days of my life.*

After you finish saying this, begin to praise the Lord, thank Him for coming into your life!

The next important thing for you to do is to receive from the Lord what is called the "Baptism of the Holy Spirit." It is very important to be filled to overflowing with the Spirit of God. You must go to the Lord in faith (believing His Word) the same way you received Jesus (and the same way you receive any promise of God). Luke 11:9-13 tells us we are going to have to go after (or receive) the things of God. They don't just come to us automatically because we've made Jesus our Lord.

⁹ "So I say to you, ask, and it will be given to you; seek, and you will find; knock, and it will be opened to you. ¹⁰ For everyone who asks receives, and he who seeks finds, and to him who knocks it will be opened.¹¹ If a son asks for bread from any father among you, will he give him a stone? Or if he asks for a fish, will he give him a serpent instead of a fish? ¹² Or if he asks for an egg, will he offer him a scorpion? ¹³ If you then, being evil, know how to give good gifts to your children, how much more will your heavenly Father give the Holy Spirit to those who ask Him!"

The Lord is assuring us that when we ask God for something He will give us exactly what we asked for.

The Holy Spirit came to earth on the day of Pentecost. Acts 2:4 says, "And they were all filled with the Holy Spirit and began to speak with other tongues, as the Spirit gave them utterance." The Holy Spirit is still here today and is waiting on believers to ask Him to fill them. It is important to remember that as you pray, you are not going to rely on "feelings." You are going to receive because you have faith in what God has said.

When you are baptized in the Holy Spirit the evidence of that experience is receiving a "prayer language." It is a way for your spirit to communicate with the Spirit of God. It is needed because there are things within God's Spirit and our own spirits for which there are no words in our native language. As you pray this prayer to receive the baptism of the Holy Spirit, prepare to yield to the utterances that are within you.

Now say this prayer out loud …

Dear Heavenly Father, I am a believer. I am Your child and Jesus is my Lord. I believe in my heart that Your Word is true. I give You my spirit, my soul and my body. Your Word says if I ask I will receive, so I am asking You to fill me to overflowing with Your Holy Spirit. I have asked and Your Word says I've received and I thank You! Now Holy Spirit, I thank You for giving me the utterance that is my prayer language. Thank You that I can now pray mysteries (Your perfect will) to the Father. (I Corinthians 14:2).

With your mouth begin to thank and praise God for filling you. As you do, certain syllables and words will rise up from within you. Stop speaking English (or your native tongue) and by faith step out boldly and speak with your new Heavenly language. (You must be willing to speak – the Lord won't force you to do it).

You are now a "Spirit-filled" believer. Pray in your new language every day. It is a gift from God that enables us to speak "heart to Heart" with our Father. Remember, the Holy Spirit is always with you. He is your Comforter, your Counselor, your Helper, your Intercessor and your Strengthener. Oh, how we need Him in the complex and dangerous world in which we live.

One important step you need to take early on in your walk with the Lord is to be water-baptized. This is to let the world know publicly that you are a part of the Body of Christ. This is also a way for you to identify with the death, burial and resurrection of our Lord. Water-baptism is the *outward sign* of the *inward work of grace* that was imparted to you when you asked Jesus to be the Lord of your life.

Finally, make sure you ask the Lord to lead you to the church He wants you in. He will lead you to one that teaches the *uncompromising Word of God!* Become a part of what is happening there. Hebrews 10:25 admonishes us to be in fellowship with like-minded believers, "not forsaking the assembling of ourselves together, as *is* the manner of some."

As you go forth now the Word says you are a "new creature in Christ". Leave your past behind. Look only to the Word to find out "who you are" now that you are a Christian. Look only to

God to find out what your future holds. Jeremiah 29:11-13 (NLT) assures us that our future will be bright and that our Heavenly Father will be right there in the middle of it all:

> [11] For I know the plans I have for you," says the LORD. "They are plans for good and not for disaster, to give you a future and a hope. 12 In those days when you pray, I will listen. [13] If you look for me wholeheartedly, you will find me.

In Conclusion

The principles of God's Word that I have shared in this book are just a portion of what God would want you to know. Through continued study of the Word, your fellowship with the Lord in daily prayer, and the leading of the Holy Spirit, you will experience an increasing knowledge and understanding of God's Kingdom and how it works. Then you, too, will be able to rejoice, knowing as I do that we are truly *walking with our King!*

Printed in the United States
By Bookmasters